W9-BNJ-899

Tiger Woods

By Alan Trussell-Cullen

DOMINIE PRESS

Pearson Learning Group

Dominie
Press

Pearson Learning Group

1-800-321-3106
www.pearsonlearning.com

Table of Contents

Chapter One
Where Did It All Begin?...........................5

Chapter Two
The Toddler Golfer 10

Chapter Three
The News Begins to Spread..................13

Chapter Four
A Full Set of Clubs 18

Chapter Five
I Do It with All My Heart 20

Appendix..26

Glossary 28

Chapter One
Where Did It All Begin?

Tiger Woods was born on December 30, 1975. His father, Earl, is African-American. His mother's name is Kutilda, and she is Thai. Earl was in the Army when he met Kutilda in Vietnam and later married her. A Vietnamese soldier with the nickname "Tiger" once saved Earl's life. So when Earl and Kutilda's little boy, Eldric, was born, Earl gave him the same nickname, "Tiger."

Tiger showed both an interest and a talent for golf early on. He has succeeded at every level and has won many tournaments—more than many other golfers who are twice his age. But it isn't just his talent that has made him successful. He works hard and he studies hard in order to make better shots and win more tournaments.

Earl Woods took up golf while he was in the Army. When he left the Army, shortly before Tiger was born, he decided to continue to improve his game. To improve his swing, he put up a net in his garage and practiced hitting golf balls into the net.

A young Tiger Woods competes in a junior golf tournament

When Tiger was six months old, Earl took him out to the garage with him. Tiger would sit in his highchair and watch for hours. He was spellbound by what his father was doing. He was so spellbound that when his mother came to feed him, he would refuse to eat if his father was about to hit the ball!

At that age, most babies are happy with a rattle or some kind of doll to play with. But Tiger was different. He was fascinated by the game of golf, so his dad took a golf putter and cut the handle to bring it down to baby size. Tiger was delighted with his new toy.

By the time he was nine months old, Tiger was beginning to walk. But he was still happy to sit for hours and watch his father hit golf balls into the net.

Then one morning, something

amazing happened.

Tiger's father had been hitting golf balls for some time, and he was tired. He sat down to take a rest. The nine-month-old toddler stood up. He picked up his cut-down putter and waddled over to the golf balls. He gave his club a waggle the way his father always did, looked at the target, swung his putter, and hit the ball perfectly into the net!

Tiger's father was so stunned, he nearly fell off his chair. The amazing golf career of Tiger Woods had begun.

Chapter Two
The Toddler Golfer

As Tiger was growing up, he was given all the usual toddler's toys. In those days, Spiderman was a big hit with kids, so Tiger had a Spiderman toy. He also had blocks and a Raggedy Ann.

But as a one-year-old, his favorite toy

was still the cut-down putter his father had given him. His favorite game was his own version of golf. He spent hours hitting a tennis ball up and down the hallway, using a vacuum cleaner pipe.

When he was eighteen months old, his father took him to a driving range for the first time—but Tiger didn't go to watch the other golfers practicing. He took along his own cut-down putter. He hit a bucketful of balls down the range, like all the grown-up players. And then, unlike most of the other players, he went home for a bottle of milk and a nap.

Shortly afterward, his father took him to a real golf course and let him play his first hole. The hole was 410 yards away, and it was a par-4 hole, which means most adults would need about four shots to get the ball into the hole. At eighteen months old, Tiger managed to do it in eleven shots.

Earl and Tiger Woods celebrate Tiger's win in a junior golf tournament in 1991

Chapter Three

The News Begins to Spread

News of this amazing young golfer started to get around. When Tiger was two years old, a TV camera crew showed up to film him playing golf. The resulting footage was broadcast on the evening news.

"This young man is going to be to golf what Jimmy Connors and Chris Evert are to tennis!" declared the reporter.

As a result of the news item, Tiger was invited to appear on "The Mike Douglas Show," where he got to putt against Bob Hope.

In the same year—remember, he was still only two years old—he played in his first golf competition against boys age ten and under. And he won!

Tiger's love of golf continued to grow. Even when he was only three, he would spend hours at it. In a television interview, he was asked why he was so good at playing golf. The three-year-old Tiger replied, "Practice."

Since most people who play golf are adults, most golf courses were not very happy about the idea of a child showing up to play there. When Tiger turned four, his mother went looking to see if she could find a golf course for Tiger to play. Eventually, she discovered one—the Heartwell Golf Park, in Long Beach, California—and a coach who was prepared to instruct Tiger. The coach was Rudy Duran. He was amazed at the young Tiger's skill.

"I was blown away," Rudy said. "He was awesome!"

When he was five years old, Tiger appeared on the TV show "That's Incredible." People were astounded by this young boy's golfing skills. But Tiger's parents were very careful to make sure he didn't let all this attention go to his head.

There were other incredible children on the show, including a young girl who was an amazing weightlifter—she hoisted up all three of the show's adult presenters! After the show, Tiger's father asked Tiger if he thought he could do what she had done.

"No way!" said Tiger.

"That's right," said Tiger's father. "She's special at weightlifting, and you're special at golf. It's good to be special at something, but it's important to remember that there are lots of other special people in the world, and lots of things other people are special at."

Tiger Woods practicing his short shot

Chapter Four
A Full Set of Clubs

Tiger had been playing golf with a set of three golf clubs. But when he was five years old, his parents decided he needed something more like a full set of clubs. However, the set didn't include a 1-iron. One day Tiger turned to his coach and said, "Rudy, how come I don't have a 1-iron?"

His coach patiently explained that he didn't think Tiger was big enough to hit the ball properly with a 1-iron. The next day, Tiger was out playing with Rudy. He reached into his coach's golf bag and took out his 1-iron. He hit the ball perfectly with it, much to Rudy's amazement. Then he did it again. And again. So what did Tiger's coach do? He got him a 1-iron!

Chapter Five

I Do It with All My Heart

Soon it was time for Tiger to go to school. He devoted himself to his schoolwork with the same intense focus that he gave to golf. His mother had one hard-and-fast rule: When Tiger came home from school, he had to finish his

**Tiger Woods works hard for everything
he wants to accomplish**

homework before he was allowed to go
near a golf club!

As Tiger went through elementary
school, he continued to work hard at
golf. He practiced for long hours,
especially in the summer during the long
school vacation.

But even at this young age he knew

that golf wasn't just about hitting the ball in the right way. You had to think about what you were doing, too. That meant being positive and believing you could do it. To help Tiger think positively about his golf game, his father bought him some tapes to listen to. On the tapes were encouraging messages. Tiger played them over and over to himself.

I believe in me.

I smile at obstacles.

I focus and give it my all.

My decisions are strong.

I do it with all my heart.

But he didn't just listen to the tapes. He used the messages when he was playing to remind him how he should be thinking—and his golf game got better and better!

At the age of eight, Tiger won the

Optimist International Junior Championship. And he won again when he was nine, twelve, thirteen, fourteen, and fifteen.

At fifteen, he became the U.S. Junior Amateur Champion—the youngest ever in golf history.

Many more titles were in his future. He won the U.S. Junior Championship again when he was seventeen. He was the first golfer to win it twice. Then he won it again when he was eighteen!

By this time, Tiger was enrolled at Stanford University, and he continued to play well. At the age of eighteen, he won the U.S. Amateur Championship—and he won again at nineteen and twenty!

At the age of twenty, Tiger was ready for a life of golf. He became a professional golfer—and the rest, as they say, is history!

Nowadays, Tiger travels all around the world playing tournaments. He has become a golf superstar. Thousands of fans come to watch him. But they don't come just to see a great golfer—they come to see a great person, too.

Earl and Kutilda Woods look on and applaud during the 2002 Master's Tournament, which Tiger won for the third year in a row

What are some of the things that make Tiger so special and so successful?

- He knows what he loves doing, and he loves doing it well.

- He practices and is always ready to learn.

- He knows how to focus. He doesn't get distracted or give up.

- He sets goals for himself and works hard to achieve them.

- He inspires others to strive to achieve their goals.

Appendix

Tiger's record book so far:

- 1997 (age twenty-one): Won the Masters Tournament by an amazing twelve strokes, the widest margin ever. Became the youngest winner ever, and the first of African or Asian descent. Achieved No. 1 World ranking. Voted PGA (Professional Golfers' Association) player of the year.

- 1998: A "quieter" year, but still No. 1 World ranking.

- 1999: Won eight PGA victories, including the final four official tournaments of the year. Won the U.S. Open by a record fifteen strokes—the largest margin of victory ever recorded at a major tournament. Broke or tied a total of nine records at the U.S. Open, including the largest lead at the midway point of the tournament. Became the all-time career money leader.

- 2000: Won eleven tournaments and became the fifth player in history and the youngest ever to complete the career Grand Slam by winning the British Open. He won by eight strokes.

- 2001: Won the Masters tournament to become the first golfer to be reigning champion of all four majors simultaneously.

- 2002 (age twenty-six): Won the Masters tournament for the second year in a row, becoming only the third golfer in the history of the tournament to do so.

Glossary

Clubs – Shafts of wood—"woods"—or metal—"irons"—that have flattened parts at the base. Each club has a different purpose, depending on how far and high you want to hit the ball.

Driving range – A place where golfers can practice hitting golf balls.

Hole – A special hole in the ground where the golf ball has to end up.

1-iron – A golf club for hitting the ball a long way. A 9-iron is used for hitting the ball short distances, and the numbers between 1 and 9 are used for middle distances.

Putter – A golf club for hitting the ball gently into the hole.

Stroke – Each time a player tries to hit a golf ball with any golf club.

Vietnam – A country in Southeast Asia.